COPING

I0801607

HATE AND INTOLERANCE

ALEX NOVAK

ROSEN PUBLISHING

Published in 2023 by The Rosen Publishing Group, Inc.
2544 Clinton Street, Buffalo, NY 14224

Designer: Rachel Rising
Editor: Corona Brezina

Portions of this work were originally authored by Avery Elizabeth Hurt and published as *Coping with Hate and Intolerance*. All new material this edition authored by Alex Novak.

Library of Congress Cataloging-in-Publication Data

Names: Novak, Alex, 1976- author.
Title: Hate and intolerance / Alex Novak.
Description: Buffalo, NY : Rosen Publishing, [2023] | Series: Coping | Includes index.
Identifiers: LCCN 2022027641 (print) | LCCN 2022027642 (ebook) | ISBN 9781499473698 (library binding) | ISBN 9781499473681 (paperback) | ISBN 9781499473704 (ebook)
Subjects: LCSH: Toleration--Juvenile literature. | Hate--Juvenile literature.
Classification: LCC HM1271 .N68 2023 (print) | LCC HM1271 (ebook) | DDC 305.8--dc23/eng/20220615
LC record available at https://lccn.loc.gov/2022027641
LC ebook record available at https://lccn.loc.gov/2022027642

Manufactured in the United States of America

CPSIA Compliance Information: Batch #CSRYA23. For further information contact Rosen Publishing at 1-800-237-9932.

CONTENTS

CHAPTER 1

RECOGNIZING HATE AND INTOLERANCE

The United States is a nation of rich diversity. Americans are represented in a vast range of different categories related to race, ethnicity, national origin, gender identity, age, religion, sexual orientation, disability, political beliefs, and economic status. Diversity in communities, schools, and workplaces brings together people with a range of different perspectives and experiences. People who are comfortable with diversity are more likely to be open to innovation and novelty. People who live and work in places that lack diversity may feel uncomfortable with unfamiliar practices and viewpoints.

Intolerance is an unwillingness to accept people who are different, often because they're viewed as a threat. They might be perceived as threatening the character of the neighborhood, one's personal moral code, or the established social order. Intolerance signifies a lack of respect for other people's basic right to their own identities and values. Intolerance can cause harmful divisions between groups that see themselves as opposing each other and refuse to consider mutual understanding.

An intolerant attitude can lead to discrimination, which is illegal in many situations. Federal law protects against employers discriminating against job applicants or employee-based categories that qualify legally as a "protected class," for example, race, color, national origin, religion, sex, age, or disability. State and local governments can pass their own laws protecting against discrimination. Social media companies have taken steps to restrict hate speech on their platforms.

Despite laws and policies, hate and intolerance continue to impose a heavy cost for many Americans. Hate and intolerance can contribute to violence and other forms of intimidation and damage. The threats posed by hate and intolerance can leave vulnerable people feeling helpless, fearful, and overwhelmed.

Engaging with a diverse variety of people from different backgrounds exposes us to new ideas and ways of doing things.

THE ORIGINS OF "US" AND "THEM"

It's easy to condemn acts of hate and the attitudes that inspire those acts. But merely condemning hate doesn't do much to stop it. Condemnation without understanding can have the unfortunate result of generating even more hate. We might laugh when we catch ourselves saying something like, "I hate haters!" Of course, hate and intolerance must be called out and denounced whenever they show up, or they will grow and fester and many more people will be hurt. But to respond effectively, we have to develop some understanding of where hate comes from. Understanding hate is one of the first steps toward eliminating it.

The tendency to categorize people based on superficial characteristics is one of the most dangerous things in the modern world—but at one time in human history, this knack for quickly sizing people up was a lifesaving skill. Our prehistoric ancestors lived in small tribes, and those tribes often competed for resources, such as food and land. People who had a tendency to be a bit cautious around outsiders may well have lived longer than people who were more open and accepting. But in the modern world, sizing people up and assigning them to groups and categories—particularly the categories of "us" and "them"—and making assumptions about what those people are like can lead to hate and intolerance, and in some cases even murder and war.

People have this tendency to discriminate against people who aren't part of their group, even when the groups are based on completely meaningless categories. In the 1970s, two social-psychologists, Henri Tajfel and John Turner, developed a framework called Social Identity Theory, which helps us understand hate and intolerance.

According to Tajfel and Turner's research, the groups people belong to—such as families, sports teams, political parties, and racial groups—are what give people a sense of belonging in the world. In order to make us feel better about ourselves, we tend to inflate the status of the group we are in and devalue the status of other groups. When you think about it, most people do this in small, mostly harmless ways quite often. For example, a fan of the New York Mets baseball team might come to believe that Mets fans are somehow better (or cooler, or nicer) people than fans of the team's archrivals, the New York Yankees. Yankees fans may feel the same way about Mets fans.

Some zealous fans identify with their fellow fans and derive some personal sense of who they are and how they differ from others based on that identity.

One of the important things about Tajfel and Turner's work is that it demonstrated that in modern times, identity—not just competition for resources—is important in causing people to discriminate. In the modern world, people discriminate against others not because they truly believe those others are a threat to their source of food or some other necessity of life, but because others are a threat to their sense of self-esteem or their idea of who they essentially are.

Strong group affiliation can sometimes (though not always) lead to intolerance and even, when taken to an extreme, hate toward people who are members of other groups. As we saw earlier in the text, being cautious around people from different groups is probably a very natural part of being human, but it is no longer useful—and is even dangerous—in the modern world. In order for everyone to get along, we need to learn to avoid this natural tendency. People belong to plenty of different groups and have lots of different characteristics. Belonging to a certain group might mean a person has a certain skin color, speaks a certain language, wears a certain kind of clothing, eats a certain kind of food, or roots for a certain baseball team—but it says absolutely nothing about the intrinsic value of that person and is never an excuse to treat that person as less valuable than anyone else.

Today, many affiliations such as common interests or social activism can cut across boundaries and promote inclusion rather than intolerance.

MOTIVATED BY FEAR

Identity is a powerful motivator for discrimination, but it's not as dangerous as fear. There is an old saying that if you scratch anger, you'll find fear. And the same is almost certainly true of hate. That can be hard to believe when you notice how often the victims of hate are the least powerful members of a society or culture. But the fact is, people who hate others are very often afraid of something. It may be that they are afraid of change.

For example, when a lot of Asian immigrants move into a neighborhood that had mostly been filled with people of European descent, it may seem to some of the people who lived there first that their neighborhood is changing too fast and that might be a little bit scary. Most people get over this easily. But some people get upset because the neighborhood is different. The store on the corner that was Henry's Diner for years and years is now a Korean supermarket with strange writing in the windows and unusual fruits in the bins by the door. If other things change at about the same time and some of those changes are unpleasant—for example, the local factory shuts down and many people lose their jobs—people can begin to blame all that misfortune on the new people. "Things were fine before all those foreigners moved in," those people might say.

Most people appreciate their neighborhood becoming more diverse. It's a chance to meet new neighbors, be exposed to a new language, and experience new cultural traditions.

The German economy was crippled after World War I, leaving ordinary Germans suffering and seeking someone to blame for their wretched circumstances.

Sometimes this happens even when people aren't new but are just different in some way from most of the other people in a community.

This is in part what happened in Germany after World War I (1914–1918). The German economy was in terrible shape for a lot of reasons. World War I had left Germany in ruins; the victors of that war were demanding that Germany pay huge war reparations; high tariffs, or taxes, were imposed by the United States on imports from Europe; and a worldwide economic depression devastated the economies of all nations. Some Germans, especially members of Germany's Nazi Party, began to blame all this trouble on the Jews. Adolf Hitler, the dictator of Nazi Germany, proclaimed that the only way for Germany to become great again was to get rid of all the Jews. Of course, this resulted in the murder of 6 million Jews in concentration camps.

We often think of what happened in Nazi Germany as an anomaly—something that could never happen again. But in fact, genocides in which entire groups of people are persecuted and killed are all too common in the world. It has happened in Cambodia, Rwanda, Bosnia, Darfur, and many other places. It happens when hate gets out of hand. It may seem silly to compare an outbreak of schoolyard bullying or even websites that post vicious things about immigrants to the mass slaughter of human beings, but if we are to prevent those extreme results of hate, we have to stop hate when it is much smaller. And one of the best places to start is very close to home.

A brutal regime called the Khmer Rouge seized power in Cambodia in 1975. Over the next four years, up to three million Cambodians were executed or died of starvation

HATE AND HATE CRIMES

The Federal Bureau of Investigation (FBI) defines a hate crime as a "criminal offense against a person or property motivated in whole or in part by an offender's bias against a race, religion, disability, sexual orientation, ethnicity, gender, or gender identity." But the organization specifically states that hate itself is not a crime. Hate speech is protected under the constitutional right to free speech, subject to certain limitations, such as inciting violence or committing defamation.

When a criminal act is determined to be a hate crime, however, the penalty is more severe than it would be for a similar crime not motivated by hatred. This is because hate crimes potentially harm the entire community and society as a whole in addition to the victim.

A hate crime targets aspects of victims' identities. Victims are often left feeling vulnerable, helpless, and traumatized by the incident.

RECOGNIZING BIAS

In 2015, researchers at Utah State University studied people who had prejudices against a variety of groups (this study looked particularly at prejudices against ethnic minorities, women, homosexuals, obese people, and people struggling with substance abuse). The researchers found that people who judge and hate others have three common characteristics: they are unable to see things from the perspectives of the people they hate, they are unable to have empathy for them, and they are uncomfortable with their own emotions about being around these people. If we cannot imagine what it feels like to be someone else, the researchers found, it is much easier to hate them or be intolerant of the ways they are different from us. But perhaps the most intriguing finding of this study is that in order to overcome hate and intolerance, we have to be aware of and comfortable with our own feelings about those other people—even when those feelings aren't very nice.

In 1998, a group of scientists began a research program designed to ferret out unconscious prejudices. They designed a series of psychological tests that could determine if a person had biases or prejudices, even if that person was completely unaware of them. The research—which is still going on—has found that while very few people truly hate others, almost everyone has at least a little bit of prejudice. Some people who are very supportive of equal rights for women took the tests and discovered that they were just a tiny bit biased against women (even some women have this bias). Others who believe strongly in protecting the civil rights of LGBTQ+

Americans discovered upon taking the test that they have a slight preference for people they perceive to be straight and some discomfort with LGBTQ+ people.

These findings don't suggest that most of us are secret bigots, rather that it's perfectly normal to have a few mild biases. And knowing that we have those biases can be a very good thing: if we take a good hard look at our own prejudices, we are better able to make sure those biases don't affect our behavior in negative ways. How we deal with these perfectly natural feelings of discomfort or prejudice toward people who are different from us in some way determines whether those biases lead to hate and intolerance or understanding and kindness.

For example, even though you know that only a very small percentage of Muslims are radical extremists, you still may have a twinge of anxiety when someone you suspect may be Muslim gets on a bus with you. That way of thinking may not be cool, but it's not evil either. The key is to let yourself admit that you have those feelings and then remind yourself that they aren't logical and shouldn't cause you to be unkind to perfectly innocent strangers. If you are aware of your feelings, then you might better understand why the man gave you a funny look when he got on the bus. He may have been responding to the funny look you gave him—without even realizing you did it! Then you can smile and say, "Hello," and what may have been an unpleasant encounter will turn into a nice one.

There is another reason it's important to be aware of our own biases, even the smallest ones. When we know that we, too, have some prejudices, we can better understand the prejudices of others.

While it is essential to be aware of any potential biases against people who are typical victims of discrimination, it is also important to be aware of prejudices we might have toward other people, such as the people we may think are likely to hate or be intolerant of the people we do like.

By acknowledging how much we all have in common, we can overcome implicit biases and make progress toward eliminating hate and intolerance.

There are many reasons hate and intolerance exist in otherwise peaceful and open societies, but most of the time they all come down to a feeling of being threatened—either with literal harm (such as physical violence or loss of the means to care for oneself or one's family) or with damage to one's sense of self. When people feel threatened, they protect themselves. They put on armor, board up the windows, and close out anyone they perceive as being even a remote threat.

The information age has made many sources of fear seem closer than ever before. Stories appear on our screens as news breaks, and we're barraged with commentary within minutes. The fabric of society seems to be under threat, leaving little recourse for ordinary people. Sometimes, it's easy to blame "them"—immigrants, people from different races, LGBTQ+ people, or those with opposing political viewpoints. But lashing out with hate, intolerance, and violence only worsens the atmosphere of fear and anxiety.

During past turbulent times, people have managed to come together to accomplish positive social change. They rejected hate and aggression, instead putting their faith and willpower in nonviolent resistance.

Tolerance can be fostered through respect for diversity, freedom of expression, and collaborative effort among people from different backgrounds.

CHAPTER 2

CONFRONTING HATE AND INTOLERANCE

The 2020s opened with racial strife, an unprecedented public health crisis, and deep political rifts dividing the country. FBI statistics on hate crimes in 2020 reflected the turmoil experienced across the nation.

In a legal context, a "hate" crime does not refer to the emotion of hatred. Rather, it is a crime committed on the basis of race, color, religion, national origin, sexual orientation, gender, gender identity, or disability. Examples of federal hate crimes are assault, murder, arson, and vandalism. The Department of Justice has prosecuted hate crimes since the passage of the Civil Rights Act of 1968, which expanded protections of the landmark Civil Rights Act of 1964. Investigating and prosecuting hate crimes brings justice for the victims of the crime, and it also sends the message to the community that law enforcement will not stand for such attacks.

In 2020, the FBI investigated 8,263 hate crime incidents, nearly a thousand more than the previous year. The largest number of incidents were based on race/ethnicity/ancestry. There were 2,871 anti-Black incidents, which was a 49 percent increase since

2019, and 279 anti-Asian incidents, which was a 77 percent increase. Although incidents based on religion decreased from 2019, there were 683 anti-Jewish crimes, by far the largest number of any religion. There were 1,110 incidents based on sexual orientation and 266 based on gender identity. About 70 percent of all incidents were "crimes against persons," which include offenses such as murder and assault. About 28 percent were "crimes against property," such as robbery, arson, and vandalism.

Many hate crimes are not reported by victims, leading to a "hate crimes reporting gap." Sometimes, victims believe that the police can't help them or wouldn't care about helping them. In other cases, they fear that their attackers will retaliate and harass them further if they notify the authorities. For some victims, there is a language barrier. The FBI urges people to report hate crimes so that law enforcement will know where to devote resources to address fighting hate crimes.

The FBI urges the public to report hate crimes in order to improve prevention and to raise awareness of threats to a particular community.

RESISTANCE THROUGH NONVIOLENCE

The struggle against hate and intolerance can't be won through more hate and violence. In the early 20th century, Mohandas Gandhi devoted his life to the cause of Indian independence from Great Britain. He called for strikes, protests, and other types of peaceful civil resistance. The British sometimes responded with violence, but Gandhi urged his followers to remain peaceful, even though many other Indians who supported independence advocated rioting and other acts of violence. Gandhi was jailed several times, but his commitment never wavered. Eventually his tactics worked and India was granted its independence in 1947.

Martin Luther King Jr., who was a leader of the movement for justice and equality for African Americans, was deeply influenced by Gandhi. Before the mid-20th century, African Americans experienced tremendous discrimination and were often the targets of hate and violence, especially in the southern states. King founded the Institute on Nonviolence and Social Change, designed to teach people that this approach was not cowardice but rather strength. In a speech about nonviolent resistance, King said, "Our aim is not to defeat the white community, not to humiliate the white community, but to win the friendship of all of the persons who had perpetrated the system in the past. The end of violence or the aftermath of violence is bitterness. The aftermath of nonviolence is reconciliation and the creation of a beloved community." King also stressed that nonviolence is as much about internal attitude as external behaviors. Not only does nonviolent resistance avoid external violence, it also avoids violence of the spirit.

Martin Luther King Jr. applied Gandhi's philosophy of nonviolence and his techniques of nonviolent resistance in the long struggle for civil rights for African Americans.

African Americans still face discrimination and even today are often the victims of hate and intolerance. But the efforts of the movement that King and others led resulted in many changes in American society. Key laws, such as the Civil Rights Act of 1964 and the Voting Rights Act of 1965, protect the rights of African Americans.

Many other movements have demonstrated the practical value of fighting hate with nonviolence. In the book *Why Civil Resistance Works: The Strategic Logic of Nonviolent Conflict*, authors Erica Chenoweth and Maria Stephan examine 323 conflicts—both violent and nonviolent—that took place around the world between 1900 and 2006. They found that nonviolent movements were twice as likely to be successful as violent ones. Nonviolence is not, however, passive. In some ways, it is even aggressive. Nonviolent resistance demands change. But it does not use violence to achieve its ends and does not respond to hate with hate.

ROSA PARKS'S RESISTANCE

The event that is generally considered the beginning of the civil rights movement took place one December evening in 1955 in Montgomery, Alabama. Rosa Parks, a 42-year-old civil rights activist, refused to give up her seat to a white man on a segregated bus. Parks was arrested and the African American community responded by refusing to ride the city's buses. This was a peaceful protest (though the protestors themselves were often the victims of violence). Parks simply said, "No," when she was asked to move.

When she was told she would be arrested if she didn't cooperate, she said quietly, "You can do that."

Even before the day on the bus that made Parks famous, she had worked hard for justice and equality for African Americans. After the bus boycott and the court ruling that made bus segregation unconstitutional, Parks moved to Detroit, Michigan. There she continued to work for justice not only for Black Americans but for Black South Africans as well.

Rosa Parks joined the National Association for the Advancement of Colored People (NAACP) in 1943 and served as the secretary of the Montgomery chapter

MALALA YOUSAFZAI'S ACTIVISM

Malala Yousafzai was born in the town of Mingora in northwest Pakistan in 1997. When she was still a child, the Taliban, a militant Islamist group, took over the area. The Taliban banned television and music, and women were forbidden to go out shopping. They shut down many schools, especially schools for girls. When she was only 12, Malala began writing a blog about what the Taliban was doing to her community, their plans to close her school, and her fears that she would be killed. She wrote under a pseudonym so that the Taliban couldn't find her and kill her, but she continued to speak out and eventually her identity became public. Nevertheless, she wrote and spoke out, arguing that all girls and women had a basic right to an education.

Malala continued to go to school, along with other girls, and did not give in to the Taliban's pressure or the many death threats she received. One day on her way home from school, a Taliban gunman boarded the bus and shot Malala in the head. Badly injured, she was rushed to England for surgery. She survived, and she still speaks out for women's right to an education.

Malala Yousafzai was awarded the Nobel Peace Prize in 2014, when she was only 17 years old—the youngest person ever to receive the honor.

REJECTING HATE

The practice of fighting hatred with nonviolence still serves as a potent act of resistance to the present day. In the fall of 1993, white supremacists began rampaging in the small town of Billings, Montana. They painted "Die Indian" on the homes of Native Americans, vandalized Jewish cemeteries, and harassed worshippers at a Black church. Then on December 2, someone threw a concrete block through the upstairs window of a Jewish home during the celebration of Hanukkah. The block destroyed a menorah belonging to five-year-old Isaac Schnitzer.

The people of Billings responded forcefully and peacefully to this wave of hate during the holiday season. They held vigils for peace, and hundreds of people teamed up to repaint houses that had been defaced. Then people all over town—very few of whom were Jewish—bought menorahs or photocopied pictures of menorahs they found in books and displayed them in the windows of their homes and offices. When Isaac's mom drove the little boy through town to show him all the beautiful menorahs, he asked if all these people were Jewish too. His mother told him, "No. They are friends."

A local store posted a sign that said "Not in Our Town. No Hate. No Violence. Peace on Earth." The words sent a powerful message to victims of hate that their friends and neighbors care, and to perpetrators of hate that their words and actions will not be accepted.

Since the Billings incidents, the phrase "Not in our town" has become a rallying cry for communities all across America when hate erupts in their midst.

ASIAN AMERICAN HATE CRIMES

In 2020, the COVID-19 pandemic swept across the world, upending people's everyday routines. For many Asian Americans, the pandemic brought threats and fear into their lives as well. The pandemic was one factor—many people, even political leaders, have referred to COVID-19 as the "Chinese virus" or the "Wuhan virus." Rising tensions between the United States and China have also aroused attitudes of hate and intolerance toward Asian Americans, regardless of nationality or ethnic origin. Violent incidents have left some Asian Americans afraid to leave their homes or send their children to school.

In March of 2021, a gunman killed six Asian American women in Atlanta, Georgia—the most extreme incident of violence during a period that saw an unprecedented increase in hate crimes against Asian Americans. The Center for the Study of Hate and Extremism found that hate crimes against Asian Americans soared by 339 percent in 2021, reaching record levels in major cities such as San Francisco and New York City. More than a third of all Asian Americans have personally experienced racism in their daily lives.

Lawmakers have taken steps to address anti-Asian-American hate crimes. The COVID-19 Hate Crimes Act, passed in May 2021, includes measures to help Asian Americans, such as increased resources for hate crimes investigations and Asian language resources. Some states have begun requiring that Asian American history be included in school curricula in order to increase awareness of Asian American contributions.

As hate crimes against Asian Americans spiked, many contended that local officials could take more effective action to address the violence.

STANDING UP AGAINST HATE

The philosophy of nonviolent resistance is also useful when confronting hate and intolerance whenever we encounter it, even if that is just in the lunchroom. If you are a victim of hate and intolerance or a witness to it—whether those acts are large ones, like what happened in Billings, or small ones, such as rudeness or insulting comments—there are concrete actions you can take. The first step is to do something. Hate and intolerance thrive when they are ignored or accepted. Telling perpetrators of hate, "not in our neighborhood, not in our school, not on our team," can stop hate in its tracks.

Acts of hate and intolerance must always be reported. If it happens at school, tell a teacher. If it happens in the community, tell a trusted adult. But it's also important for individuals to speak up on the spot when they witness or are the victims. This doesn't have to be confrontational. When someone tells a racist or sexist joke, you can simply say, "I didn't think that was funny. It is hurtful to many people." If you are a member of the targeted group, you can say, "That was hurtful. Please don't make jokes about me and my people."

It is important to stand up to such comments even when no one of the targeted group is around. Ignoring hurtful comments and behavior signals that you are okay with it as long as no one who might be offended is around. Hate and intolerance thrives and grows in the shadows until people are brave enough to say these things out loud.

You can also speak up by modeling kindness and love. Showing respect for others can quickly spread and become the norm in a school or neighborhood. Many people who practice intolerance do so not because they have strong feelings against particular groups, but because that's simply the way they've seen others behave. Sadly, intolerance can often become a habit when people repeat what they hear others say and adopt those attitudes without carefully thinking them through. Using non-offensive language and making friends with all the people in your school and community will set examples for others without having to preach or lecture. When confronting intolerance and hateful language, it can be very helpful to approach the problem with kindness. Instead of saying, "You are a mean person" or "Racists are ignorant!" you might instead say, "I think it's cool to treat everyone with respect" or "I deserve to be treated with respect."

By nudging the culture of your school or community away from hate and intolerance and toward acceptance and inclusiveness, you can make a real difference.

When a hate incident happens—say some kids painted racist slurs on a wall of the school—rather than confronting the people who defaced the wall, instead get together a group of classmates and neighbors (as many as you can find) and wash and repaint the wall. If people are making fun of a disabled classmate as he sits alone at lunch, get together several other kids and join him at his table. If you're the victim of these kinds of acts, reach out for help and support. Though it may not always seem that way, there are more good people in the world than bad.

There are also a few organized practices schools often use that can help create a culture of kindness rather than intolerance. Mix It Up at Lunch Day is an event sponsored by Learning for Justice (a program of the Southern Poverty Law Center) and held on the last Tuesday of October each year. It's simple: students who participate connect with someone new at lunch by moving from the place where they normally sit to another spot. It's a very gentle way to break down social barriers and to make new friends.

You might also consider taking part in the Great Kindness Challenge, a week in which people try to commit as many acts of kindness as possible. You can focus especially on acts that defuse hate and intolerance. The national Great Kindness Challenge is typically observed in the last week of January (you can find out more at thegreatkindnesschallenge.com), but schools can do it whenever it is convenient, and individuals can do it every day. Of course, it is crucial to not put yourself or anyone else in harm's way. But there are safe and effective actions you can take.

Remember that hate and intolerance often have their roots in fear and ignorance. Take action to correct misapprehensions about marginalized groups. Instead of retorting angrily to offensive statements, point out that many of the fearmongering stories spread on social media are sensationalized and exaggerated. Join projects promoting awareness of the hardships faced by minority groups. Take time to learn about the cultures and backgrounds of your peers and appreciate the diversity they represent.

A diverse student body encourages students to challenge stereotypes and build relationships with people with different backgrounds and beliefs from themselves.

MYTHS & FACTS ABOUT HATE AND INTOLERANCE

MYTH: Bigotry is just a part of being human. There is nothing we can do to change that.

FACT: Though it is true that humans have a natural tendency to classify people into groups and to see those groups as "us" and "them," it is by no means impossible to get over this tendency. Humans are influenced by their minds and their cultures as well as by their genes. That's why it is so important to examine these prejudices so that we take charge of our behaviors rather than letting our behaviors be in charge of us.

MYTH: The election of Barack Obama, the nation's first Black president, means that racism in America is over.

FACT: While the election of the first African American president of the United States was a major step for the United States, it did not signal an end to racism. As wonderful as it is that more African Americans, LGBTQ+ citizens, and other minorities are serving their country in elected offices both locally and nationally, members of these communities are still not being treated equally throughout the nation, and patterns of intolerance and incidents of hate continue.

MYTH: Challenging bigotry is just another form of bigotry.

FACT: People who are members of majority groups in society often claim that when minority groups demand equal rights, they are demanding special privileges and thus infringing on the rights of the majority group. However, the demand to be given the same rights, respect, and dignity as anyone else is not a demand for special treatment; it is a demand for equal treatment. No one's rights are being infringed upon when every person is given equal rights and respect.

Young people who are brought up to value multiculturalism won't just promote tolerance of diverse groups—they'll appreciate and celebrate these differences.

CHAPTER 3

ONLINE HATE AND INTOLERANCE

The early creators of the internet believed that they were creating a utopia—a place in which people would have the means to communicate and share information instantaneously. In a way, this vision has come true. Ordinary people today spend hours of their day connected to other people physically distant from themselves and to apps with no presence in the real world. We can virtually attend events across the globe. We can forge close friendships with people in other countries whom we never meet offscreen. The world's knowledge is at our fingertips in the search bar.

But the inventors of the internet did not anticipate that the anonymity permitted online would sometimes bring out the worst in humanity. People are willing to make hateful statements online that they would never utter in person. Nobody could have anticipated the consequences of the rise of social media. Facebook and other platforms are great for keeping in touch with family and friends, but they have also inflamed divisions and provided the means of spreading hate and disinformation. At worst, hate speech on social media can contribute to real violence.

Like any technology, the internet can be used for good or ill. Without the internet, the outside world would not have known about Malala Yousafzai and her struggle to protect the rights of girls to an education. Many acts of hate and intolerance would only be known to the few people who are directly affected, making it harder for the rest of the world to help.

Being a responsible online citizen can tip the power of the internet from those who use it to spread hate to those who use it to promote acceptance and inclusion.

ONLINE TOXICITY

The obvious solution to online hate is to ban it. But as we have seen, that is not necessarily a good idea. Free speech is an essential feature of democracy and is vigorously protected in many nations, including the United States and Canada. Imposing limits on the freedom of citizens to express themselves can quickly go from protecting citizens from hate to giving the haters a powerful tool to restrict the voices of those who disagree with them. At times when even people at the highest levels of government are engaging in and spreading hate speech, it becomes even more important to protect the rights of anyone to speak up freely and without fear of reprisal. Limiting the rights of those we disagree with all too often ends up limiting our own rights.

Chances are, you've encountered hate speech online. You open your Facebook or Instagram account and find a racist joke, a swastika, or a post that demeans immigrants or threatens Muslims. What do you do? Do you respond with a well-reasoned argument for why you find this offensive? Do you unfriend or block the person who made the post?

If the post is truly hateful, you can and should flag it. Most social media sites have a means for flagging offensive posts and a procedure for reviewing these. If they are deemed truly offensive, the post is deleted, and, in extreme cases, the poster's account may be suspended or canceled. If you are personally threatened by someone online or feel that you are in danger of being harmed, immediately report this to the site where the threat was posted, inform a trusted adult, and if the threat is specific, call the police. If you see something online that promotes violence or serious destruction of property, you can report it to Fight Against Hate, at fightagainsthate.com.

Social media sites, such as Facebook, Twitter, and Instagram, have policies and tools in place to restrict online hate speech.

Blocking or unfriending those you merely disagree with is not always the best approach. These days many people live in what experts call "information bubbles." They see only the opinions they already agree with, which can put up more walls between people and keep us from learning about each other. If people are simply spewing hate, then by all means report and block them. But when people are expressing opinions that are merely different from yours, it might be valuable to hear them out—even if those opinions offend you in some cases. It's never a good idea to listen to or pass on nasty posts, but if someone voted for a different candidate, is a member of a different political party, or identifies with a different religious group, then keeping the channels of communication open is always a good idea.

COUNTERING ONLINE HATE SPEECH

Another way to fight hate online is by countering it with better messages. You don't have to respond directly to, say, a racist joke or a post demeaning immigrants or LGBTQ+ people. Just find some positive information about the issue and post that. The American Civil Liberties Union (ACLU) placed an ad in Times Square that showed a Muslim woman in a hijab in front of a building painted with graffiti saying, "Muslims, go home." The image was followed by images of people holding signs that said, "Support Freedom of Religion," "Love Thy Neighbor," and the message "Fight Hate Speech with More Speech."

Good messages can go viral just as easily as hateful messages, and the impact can be just as strong. In their book *Viral Hate: Containing Its Spread on the Internet*, Abraham Foxman and Christopher Wolf tell the story of a post that appeared on Facebook in 2010 announcing a new event to take place over two weeks that July. It was "Kill a Jew Day," which encouraged followers to commit acts of violence toward Jews wherever they saw them. Followers of the site responded with many hate-filled, anti-Semitic rants and screeds (long speeches or writings).

Individuals can use their social media accounts to fight hate speech by posting positive, encouraging messages.

Facebook responded to complaints and disabled the page. (Speech that incites violence is not protected by the U.S. Constitution or Canada's Charter of Rights and Freedoms.) But before that process was complete, the Facebook community mounted a response of its own, fighting hate speech with more speech. Another event page was quickly posted. This one was "One Million Strong Against Kill a Jew Day." Responses like this are actually quite powerful. They show in no uncertain terms that there is more love than hate in the world and that for every hateful post there are millions of people who will stand up and speak out against it.

FAKING THE NEWS

Fake news has been around a long time, but the internet enables disinformation to reach huge numbers of people almost instantaneously. Social media sites are trying to crack down on fake news sites, but the best way to protect yourself from fake news is to learn how to tell truth from fiction. A few techniques can help you sort fact from fiction on the web.

Your teachers probably tell you to cite your sources when you make claims in a research paper. Demand the same of the stories you believe or share online. First find out where the news came from. Was it a legitimate news source, such as the *Washington Post*, the *New York Times*, or your hometown paper? They also print and post opinion pieces—articles that go beyond just reporting the facts and include the author's opinion and the facts. But even these authors are required to back up their opinions with verifiable facts.

When a reputable news source makes a mistake in a story, the editors publish a correction as soon as the error is discovered.

Sometimes it is not so obvious if a news outlet is legitimate or not. "Trump Orders All White House Phones Covered in Tin Foil" was a headline that ran in the "Borowitz Report," an online column that is hosted by the *New Yorker*, a very reputable magazine. But if you look closely, you'll see that at the top of the page where the article appears, it says "Satire from the Borowitz Report."

Always be sure to read the entire article before you share it on social media. Often attention-getting headlines are designed just to get you to repost them and the content is more nonsense than not. If you're still suspicious that an article may be bogus, use Google or another search engine to find out more about the author. Is it a legitimate journalist or expert? Or does this name appear at the top of yet more sketchy-looking articles and on more questionable sites? When you read the article, look for misspelled words and poor grammar. Use your critical thinking skills to determine if the writer's argument makes sense. When possible, double-check the facts.

It can be difficult to recognize our own biases. We all have them, however, and we all tend to believe posts and news items that support our biases ("I knew it all along") and reject those that don't ("oh, that's rubbish!"). Acknowledging your pre-existing beliefs can keep you from being suckered by false news stories that support those beliefs.

One way to inoculate yourself against fake news is to be very well informed. Find a source of news that you trust (preferably one that does not have a strong bias in any direction) and read it regularly. Being familiar with real news (and the conventions of real reporting) will make it easier

An exciting (or outrageous) headline might grab your attention, but the article that follows might not be what you expected—or would want to share.

to spot the fake kind. Legitimate news sources will typically list their physical location, the names of their editors, and contact information somewhere on their websites. The more you practice evaluating news, the better you'll get at spotting the fakes. But when you're not sure, there are several reputable sites that fact-check news stories and information making the rounds on the web. Snopes.com, politifact.com, and factcheck.org may have already confirmed or debunked an item you're wondering about. Abraham Lincoln really didn't say, "Half of what you read on the internet is a lie," but if he had lived long enough to see the internet, he might have.

The ways that people use the internet are constantly changing. Apps, games, and social media platforms become trendy and then wane in popularity. Likewise, when individuals and groups advocating hate and intolerance are made unwelcome on one site, they migrate to a different host. There's no easy solution to the proliferation of hate speech and toxicity on the internet. Advocating civility and tolerance during your own online activities is a solid contribution to the cause.

10 GREAT QUESTIONS TO ASK A SOCIAL MEDIA EXPERT

1. Many of my friends on Facebook post bigoted material, but they pretend they're just jokes. How can I respond?

2. My parents are naturalized citizens who were born in Iran. I keep seeing posts online that make me fear for their safety. Do I have to wait until we are actually threatened to do something?

3. I have flagged inappropriate content on several social media sites, but it doesn't seem to block offensive material. Will we ever be able to put a stop to this?

4. When I see hateful posts online, I immediately unfriend the person who posted it. Isn't it better to just ignore this kind of thing rather than respond?

5. I've been reading a lot about an increase in hate speech and hate crimes, but I haven't seen any of it personally. Is this being overblown?

6. Everyone is warning me about fake news—how can I verify the accuracy of a story?

7. The person who shares the most hateful material on my social media feed is my grandfather. How can I convince him that I don't like this stuff?

8. My school installed filters on the computers we use to access the internet—do the filters violate our rights?

9. I want to do more about hate online than just flag, block, and unfriend. How can I make a positive difference?

10. After five minutes online, I get totally discouraged about the state of the world. How can I maintain a balanced perspective while engaging online?

Promoting civility on social media might sometimes seem like a futile effort, but holding platforms accountable for users' hate speech is a good start.

CHAPTER 4

MOVING FORWARD

The United States is a nation that celebrates its diversity—mostly. A majority of Americans consider racial and ethnic diversity to be positive for the country, according to a 2019 Pew survey. Seventy-seven percent reported that they thought diversity was very good or somewhat good, while just 6 percent viewed it as bad. Many respondents—47 percent—reported that a diverse population creates challenges for policymakers; 45 percent said that it didn't make much of a difference. Three-quarters of Americans considered it important for companies to promote a diverse workforce, but the same number also thought that race should not be considered as a factor in hiring employees, even if it would increase diversity. In considering day-to-day interactions, relatively few people reported having "a lot" of interactions with people of different race or ethnicity than themselves.

It's easy to be overwhelmed by the hate, intolerance, and violence that tends to dominate news headlines. When you investigate further, though, you'll find that you're not alone in your rejection of hate and acts of violence. Most ordinary people are horrified by extremist expressions of hate and intolerance, and the people advocating and acting on these views do not represent the thoughts and feelings of the general population.

Diversity is an intrinsic part of the fabric of American society. Most people value the innovation and cultural contributions made possible by a diverse citizenry.

There have always been periods in history that have experienced outbreaks of bigotry. For example, in the years just after World War I, the United States withdrew into dangerous isolationism, nativism, and religious fundamentalism. Hate groups flourished. The Ku Klux Klan, which was formed at the end of the Civil War, had died out by the 1870s but was resurrected in 1915. The group made a powerful comeback, becoming very active in the 1920s not only in the rural South but also in many cities around the nation. This time it targeted Catholics, Jews, and immigrants as well as African Americans. What today we would call hate crimes increased dramatically in those years. While hate and discrimination never ended, the 1930s and 1940s saw a great deal of progress for previously marginalized groups, laying the groundwork for the civil rights advances of the 1950s and 1960s.

Now we find ourselves in yet another period of increased hate and intolerance. This time, however, things are different. Though some people are spreading hate, even more people are standing up and challenging that hate. Western society is becoming far less accepting of intolerance and bigotry. There was a time in our society when acts of hatred and violence would very often go unremarked. Reporting such incidents was almost unheard of, and the authorities had very little reason for acting even when they were informed.

Not too long ago, bullying was considered a normal part of growing up—a rite of passage and something kids just had to deal with. Today, schools organize anti-bullying task forces, leaders enact anti-bullying policies, and teachers and administrators are trained in recognizing and responding to acts of bullying. Victims of bullying are supported and protected; they are not expected to just accept it as a part of life.

Nearly 30,000 Ku Klux Klan members gather in Chicago around 1920. The organization made a comeback in the 1920s, a period of isolationism and xenophobia.

ANTI-TRANSGENDER DISCRIMINATION AND LEGISLATION

In 2021, 57 transgender people were killed in the U.S., according to the Human Rights Campaign. The figure was greater than the record 44 violent deaths in 2020. The actual number may actually be larger because the victims are sometimes misgendered or not reported as transgender.

Trans people experience discrimination and violence at higher rates than the general population. Many trans people report being discriminated against in employment, housing, and access to medical care, and there is no federal non-discrimination law that provides trans people with legal protections.

In the 2020s, numerous state governments passed legislation restricting trans rights. Many of these laws have targeted bathrooms, student involvement in sports, gender affirming medical care for children, and school instruction related to transgender issues.

A disproportionate number of the victims of fatal incidents of violence against transgender and gender non-conforming people are women of color.

MAKING PROGRESS

In his 2011 book, *The Better Angels of Our Nature,* cognitive scientist and author Steven Pinker makes a strong case that we are living in the most peaceful time in the history of civilization. He argues that this is not an anomaly, but a trend. Pinker called the period after World War II "the long peace" and the time after the fall of communism the "new peace." Neither of these periods were or are free from war—or other kinds of violence—but as Pinker demonstrates with reams of data, they were far more peaceful than any previous period in history. Why? At least in part it is because people all over the world, but especially in the West, were championing human rights and speaking out against everyday aggressions. Pinker provides a great deal of evidence that people are much kinder and more tolerant than they've ever been.

According to psychologist Steven Pinker, humankind is continuing to become more peaceful and tolerant than during past times in history.

So how does a society prevent or reverse these outbreaks of intolerance when they occur? One way is by learning from the past. In an opinion piece that circulated widely on the web, Sabine Heinlein, a German American, tells Americans that when she was growing up in Germany, she was taught that "the reason why Adolf Hitler was able to rise to power was that no one stood up for the Jews." As a result, modern Germans are very conscious of the responsibility to keep intolerance and hate from breeding in society. Like the United States, Germany, too, is experiencing a resurgence of intolerance. Heinlein urges people of all nations to speak up and reach out when they witness or experience hate and intolerance.

Hitler might not have come to power in Germany if more people had condemned his racist rants and stood up to the extremist views of a minority political party.

BYSTANDER INTERVENTION

Sometimes people are complacent in the face of bigotry not because they don't care, but because they have no idea what to do. Fortunately, there are now groups who train people to respond to such incidents in the best way possible. A method that has been very useful for people who are witnesses, but are not the targets of acts of hate and violence, is called the Three Ds of Bystander Intervention.

The first D, distraction, is simply to try to stop the incident by creating a distraction. Say someone is calling a person insulting names in the hall at school. You could interrupt what's going on by starting a conversation with the person or doing something that grabs everyone's attention.

The second D, delegate, means getting someone else to help out. Let someone with more authority or social status know what's happening, such as a teacher or an older student or a parent. Delegating is especially important if it looks like the situation might become violent.

Delay is the third D. This actually refers to situations where you weren't around when the initial incident happened or were unable to stop it. Examples of the "delay" tactic include helping neighbors clean up after their property has been defaced or taping a welcome note to the locker of a new student who has experienced abuse because of their race, religion, or sexual orientation.

None of these tactics seem very heroic, but they are. Heroes notice when people are in trouble and they do something to help, even when that something isn't flashy.

You can respond to a problematic situation by taking personal responsibility and reaching out to help instead of standing by and assuming that someone else will take action.

FINDING YOUR VOICE

When you try to resist bigotry, it can seem like you are all alone. But in truth, people all over the world are standing up to the recent surge in hate and intolerance and making it very clear that this is no longer accepted in our society. These efforts range from small local acts of kindness and respect to huge political movements.

In 2007, in a small school in rural Nova Scotia, Canada, a ninth-grade boy wore a pink polo shirt to his first day of school. Some other boys bullied him, calling him a homosexual for wearing pink. Two older boys—in grade 12—heard about this harassment and decided, as one of them put it, "enough is enough" and organized a counteraction. The next day more than 50 students arrived wearing pink (many, hearing of the plan, wore their own pink clothing). The message of support was clear to the student who had been bullied and it was equally clear to the bullies that they had no support.

In Philadelphia, after a Jewish cemetery was vandalized, the Philadelphia Building and Construction Council announced that it would replace the damaged headstones at no charge. A local electrical workers union volunteered to install security lighting at the cemetery. A group of Christian, Muslim, and Jewish religious leaders held a press conference to denounce the acts of violence and reinforce their support for each other.

Noting that many immigrants facing deportation actually win their cases when they have legal representation, many groups have organized to raise money to pay the legal fees of these immigrants. Many lawyers have offered their services for free.

Youth movements for civil rights and other causes have helped bring about positive change in the past. Young people today continue to organize to make the world a better place.

Standing up to hate groups can be dangerous, but there are safe ways to do it. The Southern Poverty Law Center, an organization dedicated to fighting hate and bigotry, strongly advises against attending hate rallies and marches in order to protest them. Not only is that not safe, it just increases attendance at the rally. A safer and more effective response is to stage a counter rally. If there is an anti-immigrant rally in your town, organize a welcome rally at a nearby venue. If the Ku Klux Klan is marching in your town, make no attempt to interfere (it is their legal right to march), but simply organize an anti-hate march on another street. Fighting hate speech with more speech is not just an online strategy, it can be powerful in the real world as well.

As important as it is to avoid giving too much publicity to people who spread hate, it is equally important that good people know what is going on. In fact, one of the reasons so many people are standing up and speaking out against hate and intolerance is that they are more aware now when it happens. That's why it is a good idea to let the press as well as the authorities know.

For example, say someone paints swastikas and offensive language on the locker room at a neighborhood baseball field. You can gather a group of people—as many as you can find—to come out and wash the offending words and images off the wall. But call the city government and the local newspaper, too, and let them know what's going on. The press will report not only that this hateful incident happened, but also what people did about it. It will serve both as a call to action against hate and an inspiring story of how to respond.

If you're bothered by incidents of hate and intolerance, it's important that you show up and speak out to make your opinion known.

BEARING WITNESS

If we want a future that is free of hate and intolerance, we can have one. But we have to make that happen. It requires that we speak up and reach out. Martin Niemöller was a clergyman in Nazi Germany who became an outspoken critic of Adolf Hitler, though he had once been a committed nationalist. He spent the last seven years of Hitler's rule in a concentration camp. Later, he said:

First they came for the Socialists,
and I did not speak out—

Because I was not a Socialist.

Then they came for the Trade
Unionists, and I did not speak out—

Because I was not a Trade Unionist.

Then they came for the Jews, and I
did not speak out—

Because I was not a Jew.

Then they came for me—and there
was no one left to speak for me.

Niemöller's words are a powerful reminder to us all how important it is to speak up for others, and not to wait or think that if we ignore hate, it will go away. It will go away, but only if we refuse to allow it in our midst.

After the war, Niemöller admitted that it took too long for the German people, himself included, to speak out about what was happening to the Jews during Hitler's rule.

Some days, the litany of hate and intolerance in the headlines might seem inexorable. You may doubt that you can do anything to solve the issues behind hate speech and acts of violence. But you don't have to solve the problem of hate and intolerance on your own—being one small part of the solution is an important victory for tolerance and acceptance. You are not alone. There are many people out there working resolutely to fight hate and intolerance. By staying true to your own personal integrity and sense of justice for all, you can join those who are quietly promoting tolerance and inclusiveness in their daily lives.

Slogans that represent a movement are valuable in rallying others who share a certain point of view on an issue.

In joining together with others who value inclusiveness and diversity, each person brings their own unique talents, enthusiasm, and expertise toward fighting hate and intolerance.

GLOSSARY

affiliation The state of being officially a part of or connected with a group or organization.

anomaly Something that is different from what is normal, routine, or expected.

bias Prejudice; a position (well supported or not) in favor of or against something.

bigot Someone who treats members of certain groups with hatred or intolerance.

dictator A ruler who has complete control of a government and/or society, often an oppressive ruler.

empathy The ability to imagine the feelings of others.

ethnic Relating to a group of people, within a larger population, that are categorized by cultural characteristics, such as race, religion, language, or nation of origin.

fundamentalism An excessively strict adherence to the basic tenets or scriptures of a religion or ideology.

genocide The murder of a large group of people, particularly those of an ethnic group or nationality.

hijab A head covering worn by some Muslim women.

intrinsic Being a natural or essential part of something.

isolationism The policy or practice of a nation to refrain from involvement in the affairs of other nations.

nativism The policy or practice of providing the rights and interests of native-born citizens over those of immigrants.

pseudonym A made-up name used to conceal or protect the identity of someone, often a writer.

reparations Financial or other compensation made to the victors in war by the defeated nation or nations.

reprisal Retaliation, as for an insult, damages, or other harm, perceived or real.

reputable Generally held in high esteem.

satire The use of humor and exaggeration to entertain or make statements about society.

segregated Isolated, divided, or kept apart, as when races are kept separate in society.

FOR MORE INFORMATION

AMERICAN CIVIL LIBERTIES UNION

125 Broad Street, 18th Floor
New York, NY 10004
(212) 549-2500
Website: aclu.org
Facebook and Twitter: @ACLU
Instagram: @aclu_nationwide
The ACLU is a nonprofit organization dedicated to protecting and preserving individual liberties and rights guaranteed by the United States Constitution through lobbying and litigation.

ANTI-DEFAMATION LEAGUE

605 Third Avenue
New York, NY 10158-3650
(212) 885-7700
Website: adl.org
Facebook: @anti.defamation.league
Twitter: @ADL
Instagram: @adl_national
Founded in 1913, the ADL is a global anti-hate organization that combats anti-Semitism, extremism, and other forms of bigotry to work toward a just and inclusive society.

CANADIAN CIVIL LIBERTIES ASSOCIATION

400-124 Merton Street
Toronto, ON M4S 2Z2
Canada
(416) 363-0321
Website: ccla.org
Facebook, Twitter, and Instagram: @cancivlib
The Canadian Civil Liberties Association works to educate members of the public about their rights and freedoms and to achieve equality for people throughout Canada.

FREEDOM FORUM

9893 Brewers Court
Laurel, MD 20723
(202) 292-6100
Website: www.freedomforum.org
Facebook: @FirstAmendmentForAll
Instagram and Twitter: @1stforall
The Freedom Forum works to raise awareness of five freedoms—of religion, speech, press, assembly and petition—guaranteed by the First Amendment.

HUMAN RIGHTS CAMPAIGN (HRC)

1640 Rhode Island Ave. N.W.
Washington, DC 20036-3278
(202) 628-4160
Website: www.hrc.org
Facebook and Instagram: @humanrightscampaign
Twitter: @HRC
The nation's largest LGBTQ+ civil rights organization, the Human Rights Campaign (HRC) works to end discrimination and ensure equality for all LGBTQ+ people.

LEADERSHIP CONFERENCE ON CIVIL AND HUMAN RIGHTS

1620 L Street NW, Suite 1100
Washington, DC 20036
(202) 466-3311
Website: civilrights.org
Facebook: @civilandhumanrights
Twitter and Instagram: @civilrightsorg
The Leadership Conference on Civil and Human Rights unites more than 200 different organizations of different sizes in the United States to work together toward equality for all.

LEARNING FOR JUSTICE

Southern Poverty Law Center
400 Washington Avenue
Montgomery, AL 36104
(888) 414-7752
Website: splcenter.org/teaching-tolerance
Facebook: @SPLCenter
Twitter and Instagram: @splcenter
Learning for Justice is a project of the Southern Poverty Law Center that provides free resources to educators and childcare providers to promote inclusiveness and equality in the classroom.

UNITED NATIONS EDUCATIONAL, SCIENTIFIC AND CULTURAL ORGANIZATION (UNESCO)

UNESCO Headquarters
7 Place Fontenoy, 75007
Paris, France
+33 (0)1 4568 1000
Website: www.unesco.org/en
Facebook, Twitter, and Instagram: @unesco
The United Nations Educational, Scientific and Cultural Organization (UNESCO) works to build peace through international cooperation in education, sciences and culture.

FOR FURTHER READING

Baldino, Greg. *The Early History of the Gay Rights Movement*. New York, NY: Rosen Publishing, 2018.

Baldwin, James. *The Fire Next Time*. New York, NY: Penguin Random House, 2021.

Bartoletti, Susan Campbell. *Hitler Youth: Growing Up in Hitler's Shadow*. New York, NY: Scholastic, 2019.

Coates, Ta-Nehisi. *Between the World and Me*. New York, NY: Spiegel and Grau, 2015.

Davidson, Danica. E*verything You Need to Know About Hate Crimes*. New York, NY: Rosen Publishing, 2018.

Jewell, Tiffany. *This Book Is Anti-Racist: 20 Lessons on How to Wake Up, Take Action, and Do the Work*. Minneapolis, MN: Frances Lincoln Children's Books, 2020.

Klein, Rebecca T. *Transgender Rights and Protections*. New York, NY: Rosen Publishing, 2017.

Madrone, Kelly Huegel. *LGBTQ: The Survival Guide for Lesbian, Gay, Bisexual, Transgender, and Questioning Teens*. Golden Valley, MN: Free Spirit Publishing, 2018.

Robi, Jill. *Coping with Hate Crimes*. New York, NY: Rosen Publishing, 2019.

Zusak, Markus. *The Book Thief*. New York, NY: Alfred A. Knopf, 2007.

INDEX

ABOUT THE AUTHOR

ALEX NOVAK is a freelance writer who has written many nonfiction books for children and teens, many of them addressing issues teenagers face in their daily lives. She lives in New York.

PHOTO CREDITS

Photo Credits: Cover, p. 61 Jacob Lund/Shutterstock.com; Cover, pp. 1, 3-80 STUDIO DREAM/Shutterstock.com; Cover, p. 1 HIGOOD/Shutterstock.com; pp.5, 35 Rawpixel.com/Shutterstock.com; p. 7 Sean Locke Photography/Shutterstock.com; p. 9 fizkes/Shutterstock.com; p. 11 Resul Muslu/Shutterstock.com; p. 12 Sueddeutsche Zeitung Photo / Alamy Stock Photo; p. 13 wdeon/Shutterstock.com; p. 14 Casimiro PT/Shutterstock.com; p. 17 Ink Drop/Shutterstock.com; pp. 19, 51 Lightspring/Shutterstock.com; p. 21 PiercarloAbate/Shutterstock.com; p. 23 https://commons.wikimedia.org/wiki/File:Martin_Luther_King_Jr_St_Paul_Campus_U_MN.jpg; p. 25 https://commons.wikimedia.org/wiki/File:Rosaparks.jpg; p. 27 https://commons.wikimedia.org/wiki/File:Malala_Yousafzai.jpg; p. 29 VDB Photos/Shutterstock.com; p. 31 Sophon Nawit/Shutterstock.com; p. 33 DisobeyArt/Shutterstock.com; p. 37 CarlosBarquero/Shutterstock.com; pp. 39, 49 insta_photos/Shutterstock.com; p. 41 Michael Vi/Shutterstock.com; p. 43 YimJi WK/Shutterstock.com; p. 45 Kaspars Grinvalds/Shutterstock.com; p. 47 Fabio Principe/Shutterstock.com; p. 53 Everett Collection/Shutterstock.com; p. 55 Elena Tolmach/Shutterstock.com; p. 56 https://commons.wikimedia.org/wiki/File:Steven_Pinker_G%C3%B6ttingen_10102010a.JPG; p. 57 https://commons.wikimedia.org/wiki/File:Adolf_Hitler_colorized.jpg; p. 59 golubka57/Shutterstock.com; p. 63 fitzcrittle/Shutterstock.com; p. 65 https://commons.wikimedia.org/wiki/File:Ds._Niemoller_spreekt_in_Amsterdam,_Carre,_Bestanddeelnr_907-3454.jpg; p. 66 Steve Sanchez Photos/Shutterstock.com; p. 67 Prostock-studio/Shutterstock.com